Grasslands

Steck
Vaughn™

HOUGHTON MIFFLIN HARCOURT
Supplemental Publishers

www.SteckVaughn.com
800-531-5015

Grasslands

contents

Grasslands
Fact Matters

ISBN-13: 978-1-4190-5454-9
ISBN-10: 1-4190-5454-6

First published by Blake Education Pty Ltd as *Go Facts*
Copyright © 2006 Blake Publishing
This edition copyright under license from Blake Education Pty Ltd
© 2010 Steck-Vaughn, an imprint of HMH Supplemental Publishers Inc.

Printed in China

4 5 6 7 8   0940   15 14 13 12
4500363486

What Is a Grassland?

Grasslands are environments with a lot of grass.

Grasslands need 10 to 40 inches of rain each year. Grasslands would become deserts with less rain. They would become forests with more rain.

There are two main types of grasslands. They are **savannas** and **temperate** grasslands. Savannas are also called tropical grasslands.

Savannas are found in warm **climates**. They have wet and dry seasons.

Temperate grasslands have cold winters. They have warm summers with some rain. Temperate grasslands are also called **steppes** or **prairies**.

Some grassland animals jump to see above the tall grass.

Fires are common during dry seasons. This fire was in Kakadu National Park.

Did You Know?

African savannas get three times more rain than Australian savannas.

This ostrich does not need trees to make a nest.

Temperate grasslands have different soil and plants than savannas.

Temperate grasslands have deep, dark soil. Rotting grass roots hold the soil together. The roots provide nutrients for the soil. People use temperate grasslands to grow crops and **graze** animals.

There are almost no trees or large shrubs in temperate grasslands. It is too cold and dry for them to grow.

Savannas have **porous** soil. Water drains through it very quickly. The soil does not get many **nutrients** from rotting plants and animal droppings. There are trees and shrubs dotted across savannas.

African elephants create grasslands by knocking down trees.

Some grasslands are covered with water for short periods.

North American prairies are mainly used for growing crops.

Spinifex grasses grow in sandy soil. These grasses cover about 20 percent of Australia.

The Mongolian Steppes

The Mongolian steppes are dry temperate grasslands in central Asia.

Temperatures on the steppes **vary** widely. It gets as hot as 85 degrees Fahrenheit in summer. It gets as cold as minus 22 degrees in winter.

Nomads look after camels, sheep, goats, and cows in the Mongolian steppes. They travel great distances every year with their herds.

The steppes are also home to many wild animals. There are eagles, foxes, hares, and cranes.

A rare steppe animal is the Przewalski's horse. This **species** of horse almost became **extinct** when people hunted it for food. The last 31 Przewalski's horses in the world lived in zoos. In 1992 a small group of horses was released back into the wild.

a golden eagle

The steppes cover about 20 percent of Mongolia's land.

The Przewalski's horse is the national symbol of Mongolia.

Did You Know?

A camel's hump does not store water. It stores fat. The fat is an energy source. If the fat is not replaced, the hump shrinks and droops.

The Bactrian camel is used for wool, milk, meat, and leather. It has two humps.

Grassland Plants

*Grasses are not the only plants in grasslands. **Forbs**, **sedges**, trees, and shrubs grow there, too.*

There are about 7,500 species of grasses. They can survive the harsh climate of a grassland. They store food in their roots for the long dry seasons. Grasses have thin leaves. The leaves help them save water. Deep roots help stop the plants from being pulled up by animals.

Forbs are nonwoody flowering plants. Wildflowers and herbs are forbs. Shrubs and trees are woody flowering plants.

Sedges are grass-like plants that grow in fresh water. Papyri and bulrushes are types of sedges.

a seed pod from a baobab tree

Did You Know?

Elephant grass is the tallest grass in the world. It can grow 13 feet high.

Giraffes can reach the highest branches of acacia trees in Africa.

Baobab trees store hundreds of gallons of water in their trunks.

How Grass Gets Water

Some plants have one long root called a tap root. Most grasses have many small roots. What type of root is the best for getting water?

You will need:

- two pieces of cotton rope (about 4 inches long)
- two small glass jars
- water

Directions:

1 **Unravel** the end of one piece of rope. Pull half of it apart into loose threads. It now looks like grass roots.

2 Put half a cup of water into each jar. Place the piece of rope with loose ends into one jar. Count to *20* and then remove it.

3 Place the other piece of rope into the other jar. Count to *20* and then remove it.

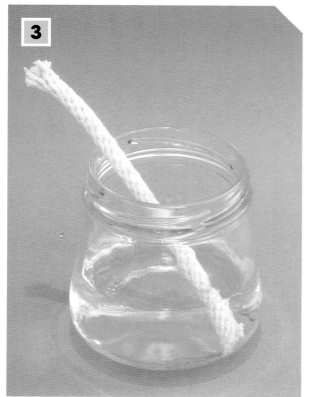

Measure the amount of water left in each jar.

Many thin threads soak up more than one thick rope. This is the way grasses **absorb** water.

Grassland Animals

Grasslands are home to many different animal species.

African grasslands hold the biggest herds and greatest variety of hoofed mammals on Earth. They hold 72 of the world's 84 species of antelopes. Some of these are the eland, impalas, gazelles, oryx, and kudu.

Up to 16 grazing species may share the same area. They eat different parts of the grass plant. This helps the plant regrow. In African savannas, zebras eat the longest parts of the grass. Antelopes follow and eat the grass shoots. Animal droppings help to **fertilize** the soil.

Termite mounds up to 13 feet tall are common in the savannas of Africa and Australia. In Mongolia, eagles nest on the ground because there are no trees.

Dung beetles like to eat animal droppings.

Kangaroos are common in Australian grasslands.

American bison have excellent **senses** of smell and hearing. But they have poor eyesight.

Did You Know?

Cheetahs are the fastest land animals in the world. They can run 70 miles per hour.

Savanna Seasons

*African savannas have **cycles** of wet and dry seasons.*

1 Dry season

Hot winds begin to blow. Grasses die at the surface. Grass roots remain alive. Fires may burn whole areas. Water holes dry up. Many animals are forced to **migrate**. There are thunderstorms before the wet season starts.

2 Wet season

When the rains start, grasses can grow an inch in one day. Rivers run again. Water holes refill. Many animals give birth when there is plenty of food. The rain may last for months or only weeks.

3 Return to dry season

The grassland begins to dry out again after the rains stop. The grasses are eaten or die at the surface. They will grow again when the rains return.

Animals on the Move

Millions of animals migrate across the grasslands of Africa's Serengeti Plain. Migrate *means "to move to another place."*

Wildebeests are a type of antelope that migrates. Each year more than one million wildebeests migrate 1,200 miles. They travel to find the fresh grass that grows after the rains. Thousands of zebras and gazelles migrate with them.

When the grasslands dry out, the animals move. They travel 30 to 50 miles each day. The wildebeests spend months in the northern part of the Serengeti. They then follow the rains back to the south.

Many wildebeests die during the journey. Before the migration begins again, the wildebeests give birth to calves.

The animals must cross the deep Masai Mara River.

The herds stay near water holes during the dry season.

Lions, hyenas, and crocodiles hunt the migrating animals.

Wildebeests can sense where rain is falling.

Did You Know?

The sooty shearwater has the longest migration. This seabird flies about 46,000 miles around the Pacific Ocean each year.

Does It Migrate?

Grassland animal	Is it a plant eater?	Does it migrate?	
Wildebeest	yes	yes	
Zebra	yes	yes	
Rhinoceros	yes	no	
Giraffe	yes	no	
Hyena	no	no	
Cheetah	no	no	

Glossary

absorb (ab SAWRB) to take in a liquid

climate (KLY miht) the usual weather conditions in a particular place

cycle (SY kuhl) a repeating process

extinct (ehk STIHNGKT) no longer existing; died out

fertilize (FUR tuh lyz) to spread something on soil or plants that helps plants grow

forb (fawrb) a type of nonwoody flowering plant

graze (grayz) to feed on grass

migrate (MY grayt) to move from one area to another, usually to find food

nomad (NOH mad) a person who moves from place to place

nutrient (NOO tree uhnt) anything that plants or animals use to live and grow

porous (POHR uhs) allows liquid or air to pass through

prairie (PRAIR ee) a name for a temperate grassland

savanna (suh VAN uh) a name for a tropical grassland

sedge (sehj) a grass-like plant that grows in wet places

sense (sehns) the power of the mind to know what happens; a feeling

species (SPEE sheez) a set of animals or plants with similar features

steppe (stehp) a name for a temperate grassland in central Asia

temperate (TEHM puhr iht) not very hot and not very cold

unravel (uhn RAV uhl) to separate threads; to pull apart

vary (VAIR ee) to make or be different

Index